LEARN MEDIA LITERACY SKILLS

HOW TO IDENTIFY
ONLINE SCAMS AND PREDATORS

by Marne Ventura

San Diego, CA

© 2025 BrightPoint Press
an imprint of ReferencePoint Press, Inc.
Printed in the United States

For more information, contact:
BrightPoint Press
PO Box 27779
San Diego, CA 92198
www.BrightPointPress.com

ALL RIGHTS RESERVED.

No part of this work covered by the copyright hereon may be reproduced or used in any form or by any means—graphic, electronic, or mechanical, including photocopying, recording, taping, web distribution, or information storage retrieval systems—without the written permission of the publisher.

LIBRARY OF CONGRESS CATALOGING-IN-PUBLICATION DATA

Name: Ventura, Marne, author.
Title: How to identify online scams and predators / by Marne Ventura
Description: San Diego, CA: BrightPoint Press, 2025 | Series: Learn media literacy skills |
  Audience: Grade 7 to 9 | Includes bibliographical references and index.
Identifiers: ISBN: 9781678209766 (hardcover) | ISBN: 9781678209773 (eBook)
The complete Library of Congress record is available at www.loc.gov.

CONTENTS

AT A GLANCE	4
INTRODUCTION TRICKED BY A TRADE	6
CHAPTER ONE ONLINE SCAMS	12
CHAPTER TWO ONLINE PREDATORS	24
CHAPTER THREE SPOTTING SCAMS AND PREDATORS	36
CHAPTER FOUR FINDING HELP	48
Glossary	58
Source Notes	59
For Further Research	60
Index	62
Image Credits	63
About the Author	64

AT A GLANCE

- A scam is a dishonest plan to trick people and take their money or information. Online scammers use emails, text messages, and social media posts to steal from people.

- Online predators use technology to find and harm people.

- Some scammers send messages that appear to be from trusted sources. This is called *phishing*.

- Identity theft occurs when scammers trick users into giving them account numbers or bank information. Scammers use this information to steal money.

- The internet makes it possible for online predators to pretend to be people they are not. Some create fake profiles that appeal to their targets.

- Some predators want photos of their targets. Others try to meet their targets in person.

- People can avoid scams and predators by protecting their information and staying away from people they do not know online.

- People who have fallen victim to a scam or have been targeted by a predator should talk to a trusted adult. They can also contact law enforcement.

INTRODUCTION

TRICKED BY A TRADE

Kayla logged in to her favorite game. She played the game online with her friends. She often chatted with them while playing.

Kayla's parents had gotten her in-game **currency** for her birthday. She used it to buy special clothes for her **avatar**. She bought a sword and a baseball cap. She also bought a **virtual** pet rabbit.

> More than 90 percent of teens play video games at least once a week. This puts them at risk for scams.

Many games have exclusive currency or add-ons that players can get by spending real-world money.

As Kayla played, a message popped up in the chat box. It looked like it was from her friend. Did Kayla want to trade her sword for a pet mouse? Kayla wanted a new pet. The mouse was worth way more than the sword. Kayla agreed. She clicked on the link in the chat box and made the trade. But something was wrong. The sword was gone from her inventory. But the pet mouse had not been added.

Kayla found her mother and asked for help. They saw that Kayla had been tricked.

The other player had used a name that was similar to her friend's name. But it was not her friend. The link they sent for trading was not a real link for the game. It went to a different website. Kayla's sword had been stolen. She had been scammed.

Many scams specifically target young people. Predators target this group, too.

INTERNET DANGERS

The internet has endless amounts of information and entertainment. But it also has dangers. Scams are among these dangers. Scams are tricks that fool people into giving money or private information to others. John Breyault is the director of Fraud.org. He says, "At the end of the day, scammers are after money or information they can turn into money."[1]

Online scams are becoming more common. The number of people using the internet is greater than ever. This gives scammers more potential victims.

Online predators are also on the rise. In nature, a predator is an animal that hunts other animals. On the internet, predators are people who use technology to find

Every year, one in five minors receives an unwanted sexual message online.

and hurt people. These predators often prey on young people. They might want inappropriate photos. Or they might want to hurt people in person.

There are ways to spot online scams and predators. Users can learn about scams and how they work. They can learn how to watch out for online predators. Then they can safely enjoy the benefits of technology.

CHAPTER ONE

ONLINE SCAMS

Online scammers use technology to steal from others. There are many types of scammers. But their goals are the same. They trick people to get money.

Some scammers trick users into sending money. Others trick users into giving out personal data. This data includes passwords and account numbers. Sometimes scammers use this information to take money from bank accounts.

Many teens make online purchases. Some become the targets of scams.

More than 3.4 billion phishing messages are sent each day.

Other times they sell the information to other scammers. Online scammers can cost people thousands of dollars.

PHISHING

One of the most common types of scams is called *phishing*. "Phishing is when someone uses fake emails or texts to get you to share valuable personal information," says Colleen Tressler.[2] Tressler is a consumer education specialist.

Phishing scammers are tricky. Their messages appear to be from trustworthy sources. They may pretend to be from a user's school, bank, or job. They often contain a real company's name and logo. At first glance, the messages look real.

Phishing messages often ask users to click on links. The links may prompt users to enter their usernames and passwords.

How Phishing Got Its Name

The first phishing scams occurred in the 1990s. The scams reminded people of scammers from the 1960s and 1970s called *phreaks*. Phreaks used illegal methods to make phone calls without paying. The new scam also made people think of fishing. People catch fish by luring them with bait. Online scammers lure their victims in a similar way. The new scam was labeled *phishing*.

Other times, users may be asked to enter their credit card information. This information goes to the scammers who sent the phishing email. The scammers use the information to take people's money. They shop with stolen credit cards. They might

People should ignore any posts or messages offering free money or prizes.

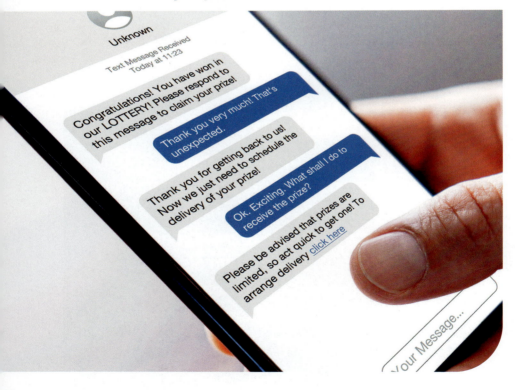

even open new accounts with people's information. This is called identity theft.

Phishing links may also download malware onto users' computers. Malware is software that damages computers. Users may be unable to use their files unless they pay a fee to the scammers. Malware can also help scammers access computer data. This allows scammers to steal private account information.

FALSE PROMISES

Many scams begin with false promises. Scammers will promise users something in exchange for a fee. Fake contests are one example of this type of scam. Scammers reach out to users. They say they are holding a contest. The scammers promise prizes in exchange for an entry fee. The user sends the fee. But they never receive a prize.

Other contests might be free to enter. They may promise to reward the best artist, model, musician, or actor. Users apply. The scammer tells them they won. The scammer tells the user to pay fees to help promote their work. In truth, there is no contest or promotion. These scams often target young people.

Young people are also the targets of scholarship scams. Some scammers advertise scholarships and grants. They tell students to pay a fee in order to be considered. They promise the students will get their fees back if they do not win the scholarship. People send the scammers money. They never hear from the scammers again.

SHOPPING SCAMS

Some scammers try to trick users into buying fake products. They make shopping websites that sell expensive-looking

Online shoppers should look for reviews before making purchases on new websites.

In 2023, scammers cost Americans $10 billion.

products for low prices. Users enter their payment information. But the purchased products never arrive.

Shopping scammers may take more than just the money people pay for the fake products. Scammers can steal the credit card information that buyers enter. They can make purchases using the stolen information.

Young people are often the victims of shopping scams. Scam expert Steve Weisman says that young people are "big online spenders for expensive goods. Often they are lured into phony websites that take their money and sell them nothing."[3] The scammers often get away with these tricks. Many young people are embarrassed about being tricked. They do not report the scams to their parents.

WHY DO PEOPLE FALL FOR SCAMS?

People fall for scams for different reasons. Many people fall for phishing scams because the messages look real. The victim trusts the person or business the message says it is from.

Scammers sometimes pretend to be law enforcement. They threaten to have the target arrested if the target doesn't send money.

Other scams work because scammers pretend to need help. They might say they need money for a plane ticket. Or they might pretend to have unpaid medical bills. The user feels sympathy for the scammer and wants to be kind. Scammers prey on this kindness.

People may also fall for scams because they are rushed. Scammers often pretend that their messages are urgent. They may say that the recipient owes money. They say the person will be in trouble if they do not send money right away. The victim rushes to pay the scammer. The user does not stop to consider that the message may be fake.

CHAPTER TWO

ONLINE PREDATORS

Online predators use the internet to hurt others. Many prey on young people. Predators have different goals. Some want to talk to people about inappropriate subjects. Others want nude or sexual images of their targets. Still others want to meet their targets in person and hurt them.

Predators have always existed. But the internet has given them new ways to strike. Ben Halpert is an online safety expert.

Online predators manipulate their targets, tricking them into doing what the predator wants.

Most young people who are targeted by online predators do not tell their parents about the harassment.

He says, "Tech has made it easier for predators to get our kids faster and more efficiently."[4] Halpert says the internet has also given predators the opportunity to hurt more people by making communication with strangers seem normal.

In 2021, the Federal Bureau of Investigation (FBI) estimated that more than 500,000 online predators were active each day. More than half of their targets were ages 12 to 15. Nearly 90 percent were contacted through online messaging services.

GROOMING

Online predators have different goals. But they generally use similar strategies. They first choose a target. They often look for

Predators often look for targets on online video games.

someone who seems lonely or unhappy. They will find people who post their feelings or problems on social media. The predators will then reach out to their target. They attempt to gain the user's trust. This process is called grooming.

Grooming may seem innocent at first. Predators will message their targets. They will offer their friendship. They say they understand. They compliment their targets. Once they have a user's trust, they slowly become inappropriate. They talk about sex. They ask for private photos. They ask the user to keep what they're doing secret.

Emma was a victim of grooming. She was 14 when her parents got her a smartphone. Emma posted on Instagram about being lonely. A man responded and

Online predators use social media websites such as Instagram to find targets and share inappropriate images.

the two began trading messages. This went on for a few weeks. He gained her trust. He made her feel less lonely. Then they made a plan to meet. He said he would meet her at her house when no one else was home. It turned out that the predator was a 22-year-old man. The predator attacked Emma and left. Emma called her parents. They took her to the hospital. The man was caught and sent to prison.

CATFISHING

Some predators conceal their true identities. They pretend to be someone they are not. This is called catfishing. Some predators make fake profiles on Facebook or dating sites. They post photos of young, attractive people and pretend they are photos of themselves. They lie about their jobs. They make up life stories that they think will appeal to their targets.

Predators often shower their victims with compliments and affection. They earn their targets' trust before asking for inappropriate images.

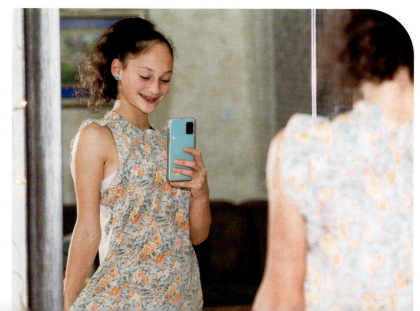

Some predators specifically catfish young people. They pretend to be people their targets' age. This helps them gain their targets' trust.

However, many predators do not catfish their targets. They are upfront about their age. But they make the target think that their relationship is normal. They say that the user is mature. They compliment the person they are grooming. They make the user think that the relationship is **consensual**. In reality, this is a form of abuse.

INAPPROPRIATE IMAGES

There are several types of online predators. Some want inappropriate images. These predators often want nude or sexual pictures of people under the age of 18. These images are called child sexual abuse material. It is illegal to possess these images. But that does not stop online predators.

Some predators collect these illegal images. Others sell them to people. Still others use these images as **blackmail**. The predators threaten to release the photos if the users do not do what they are told.

Predators do not always start by asking for inappropriate photos. They first groom their targets. They might ask for innocent pictures at first. They might request photos of what the person is doing. They might ask for images of pets or food. They request an image of the user's room. As they gain trust, they start to ask for pictures of

Some predators try to convince their targets to meet them alone.

the user. Then they begin to ask for more explicit photos.

PREDATORS IN PERSON

Some predators want to meet their targets in person. These people are especially dangerous. They may want to assault their victims. They may want to kidnap them. Some may even kill their targets.

Predators work to gain the trust of their target. Then they try to find out where the user lives. They learn about the person's habits. They know which route the user takes to school. They figure out when the person will be alone. This helps them find the user in person. Some will travel across the country to find their targets.

Sometimes predators convince their targets to come with them willingly. These predators are good at tricking people. Breck LaFave was 14 years old when he

Alicia's Law

In 2001, a 13-year-old girl named Alicia Kozakiewicz was kidnapped by a man she met online. It took 4 days for the FBI to find her. Now Kozakiewicz works to fight child predators. A law named after her, Alicia's Law, gives money to a US task force that works to stop predators.

joined an online gaming group. He knew many of the group members in real life. But the man who started the group was a stranger. His name was Lewis Daynes. Daynes groomed Breck. He said he would help Breck get a job working with computers. He convinced Breck to come to his house. When Breck arrived, Daynes murdered him.

Breck's mother, Lorin LaFave, was heartbroken. LaFave created the Breck Foundation to educate people about internet safety. She hopes to stop similar crimes from happening in the future. "I want everyone to understand that they can be groomed and hurt," LaFave says. "I cannot bear for another family to go through this."[5]

CHAPTER THREE

SPOTTING SCAMS AND PREDATORS

As the internet has changed, so have scammers. They have found new ways to steal money. Their scams continue to evolve. By learning their tricks, users can better spot scams. This can help people stay safe online.

The same is true about predators. The internet helps these criminals hide who they are. But there are signs that someone who wants to become a friend online is not

Media literacy can help teens stay safe online.

being truthful. Users who can spot these signs will be able to avoid online predators.

SPOTTING AND AVOIDING SCAMS

Some scammers use current events to make themselves look real. They might ask for money to help a country at war. They might say that a new law can help students pay off their loans. Luckily, there are ways to tell if these opportunities are scams.

People can visit trustworthy websites that warn users about new scams. Fraud.org is one such website. The website of the Federal Trade Commission (FTC) also has helpful information. The FTC is a government organization that protects people from scams and illegal business practices.

Looking closely at a message can also help users spot scams. Scam messages often have mistakes. They often

The Federal Trade Commission was founded in 1914.

39

PHISHING EMAIL

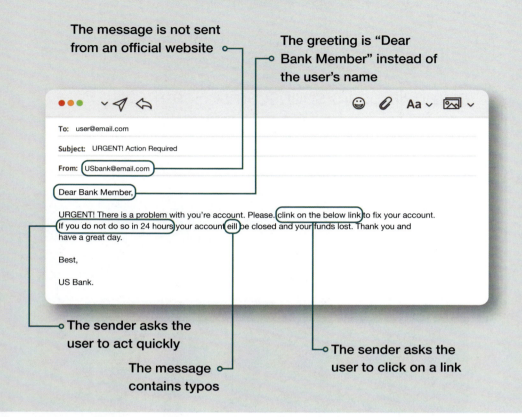

People should read emails carefully. They should look for signs that emails may be scams.

have misspellings or poor grammar. Messages pretending to be from a trusted company may have incorrect logos. They may address the recipients vaguely or by their email addresses. People should also pay close attention to the sender's email address. They should never trust messages that pretend to be from a trusted company but are not sent by the company's normal email address.

Messages announcing that the recipient has won something are likely scams. Users should avoid directly responding to these messages. They can figure out whether a prize is real by going to the company's official website. If there is no mention of a contest on the website, it is most likely a scam.

Scammers want users to think that they must act fast. That way the user will not have time to think about what they are doing. The scammer might offer a low price on something the user wants. But the scammer may say only one is left in stock.

The user must buy it now. John Breyault says, "Scammers want to create a sense of urgency. They want to get you to act, to use that animal fight-or-flight part of your brain."[6]

Peer-to-peer payment apps allow users to quickly send money to others.

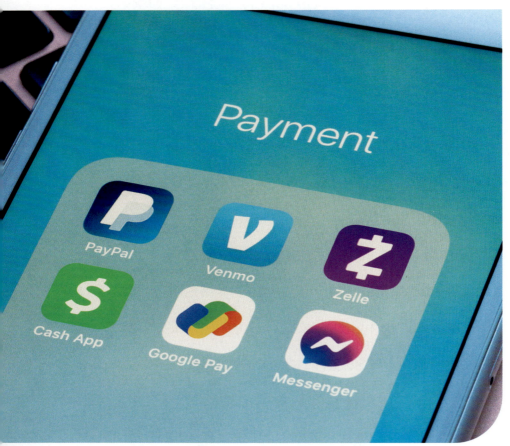

42

How someone wants to be paid can be another sign of fraud. Scammers often want to be paid with gift cards. They also use peer-to-peer payment apps. These apps include Venmo, Cash App, and Zelle. Amy Nofziger is a fraud expert. She says, "Criminals like their money fast, quick, and untraceable."[7] Peer-to-peer payment apps help scammers stay **anonymous**.

Most users can tell when something about a message does not feel right. They should trust their **instincts**. Users who get emails or text messages from scammers can block those senders. They should never give personal or financial information to people they do not know. They should resist pressure to act fast. If they are ever unsure about a situation, they should talk to a trusted adult.

SPOTTING AND AVOIDING PREDATORS

There are signs that users can look for to spot online predators. Predators are often charming. They figure out what the user likes and wants. They make the user feel important. Predators often flatter users. They ask personal questions. They say they share the same interests as the user. As time goes on, the predators share secrets. They ask the user to do the same. They might send gifts or do favors. The predator might guilt the user into doing something that makes the user uncomfortable.

Predators often tell their targets to keep their relationships secret.

People can protect themselves from online predators by watching out for people who make them uncomfortable. They should never share personal information with strangers. This includes addresses and phone numbers. They should not trust people they meet online. They can use privacy controls to prevent strangers from seeing their location. Most importantly,

Safety Tips

Many social media websites allow users to make their accounts private. This prevents people users do not know from seeing their posts. This can prevent predators from sending users messages. Users can also block anyone who makes them uncomfortable. This stops the blocked person from interacting with the user.

Social media users can report messages or accounts that make them uncomfortable.

people can talk to a trusted adult when something feels wrong. They can ask for help and advice.

CHAPTER FOUR

FINDING HELP

Scammers and online predators are good at what they do. Even the smartest people can be tricked by them. It is never the victim's fault for being scammed or hurt.

When people realize they have been tricked by a scammer or online predator, they may be embarrassed. They may feel ashamed. But there are ways for victims to find help.

People of any age or gender can become victims of online scams or predators.

People under age 20 are at the highest risk of becoming victims of online scams.

DEALING WITH SCAMMERS

The first thing people should do if they believe they have been scammed is to cut contact with the scammer. Victims should not answer the scammer's calls or messages. They should also not give the scammer any money.

Next, young victims should tell a trusted adult about the scam. This could be a parent or guardian. It could also be a teacher or counselor. Together, they should decide whether any personal information has been **compromised**. If the victim paid the scammer with a credit or debit card, the card information may have been stolen. Information could also be stolen if the scammer had access to the victim's computer or passwords.

If there is a chance that personal information was compromised, victims must take action. They should change any compromised passwords. They should also call their banks and make sure no suspicious purchases were made. If purchases were made, the victim can tell the bank they were scammed. The bank can then refund their money. Victims should also ask their banks to cancel their cards. This means no one is allowed to use the cards. The banks will send new cards.

People should report scams to their local law enforcement. They can also report scams to the FTC. The FTC looks into

Two-Factor Authentication

People can protect their data by enabling two-factor authentication on their accounts. Two-factor authentication requires those logging in to confirm their identities. This is often done by typing in a code sent as an email or text message. This prevents hackers from logging in with a stolen password. The FTC encourages people to use two-factor authentication to protect important accounts.

People can temporarily freeze their bank cards online or on their bank's app.

Social Security numbers should only be given to trusted organizations such as schools, banks, and employers.

reported scams. It builds cases against scammers. Then it brings scammers to justice. People can report scams on the FTC website.

The FTC also offers help to people whose Social Security numbers were stolen. Social Security numbers are unique numbers given to US citizens. The number allows the government to track a person's earnings. Social Security numbers also allow people to open bank accounts and get credit cards.

DEALING WITH PREDATORS

It can be scary for people to realize they have been groomed by an online predator. It can be especially frightening for young people. But no one has to deal with this situation alone.

Teens who think they may have been speaking with an online predator should immediately tell a trusted adult. The teen and the adult should then speak to law enforcement. They should not try to handle the situation by themselves. Online predators can be dangerous. Contacting the police can be intimidating. But it could help save another teen in a similar situation.

Law enforcement will likely need access to any electronic devices that were used to communicate with the predator. They may need screenshots of conversations. They may need to see any images sent between the user and the predator. Documenting this evidence can help law enforcement determine if a crime has been committed. It can also help them bring the predator to justice.

Scammers and online predators are real dangers. They can hurt people financially, emotionally, and physically. They can make people feel powerless. But there are ways people can protect themselves from these criminals. By learning to spot scams and online predators, people can stay safe online.

People can report online predators to their local police or FBI offices. They can also contact the National Center for Missing and Exploited Children.

GLOSSARY

anonymous

unknown and unidentified

avatar

an image that represents a user online

blackmail

the act of threatening someone, often by threatening to leak private information, in order to force a person to do something

compromised

exposed or put in danger

consensual

agreed upon or accepted by all involved parties

currency

a form of money

instincts

a person's unconscious feelings or responses to something

virtual

describing something that exists on the internet

SOURCE NOTES

INTRODUCTION: TRICKED BY A TRADE

1. Quoted in Heather Kelly, "Yes, It's a Scam: Simple Tips to Help You Spot Online Fraud," *Washington Post*, September 6, 2022. www.washingtonpost.com.

CHAPTER ONE: ONLINE SCAMS

2. Colleen Tressler, "Netflix Phishing Scam: Don't Take the Bait," *Federal Trade Commission Consumer Advice*, December 26, 2018. http://consumer.ftc.gov.

3. Quoted in Janet Fowler, "10 Common Scams Targeted at Teens," *Investopedia*, November 27, 2022. www.investopedia.com.

CHAPTER TWO: ONLINE PREDATORS

4. Quoted in Nellie Bowles and Michael H. Keller, "Video Games and Online Chats Are 'Hunting Grounds' for Sexual Predators," *New York Times*, December 7, 2019. www.nytimes.com.

5. Quoted in Anna Moore, "I Couldn't Save My Child from Being Killed by an Online Predator," *Guardian*, January 23, 2016. www.theguardian.com.

CHAPTER THREE: SPOTTING SCAMS AND PREDATORS

6. Quoted in Kelly, "Yes, It's a Scam."

7. Quoted in Kelly, "Yes, It's a Scam."

FOR FURTHER RESEARCH

BOOKS

Jonathan Cristall, *What They Don't Teach Teens: Life Safety Skills for Teens and the Adults Who Care for Them*. Fresno, CA: Quill Driver, 2020.

Tammy Gagne, *Online Predators.* San Diego, CA: BrightPoint Press, 2022.

J.K. O'Sullivan, *Online Scams.* San Diego, CA: BrightPoint Press, 2022.

INTERNET SOURCES

Ademolawa Ibrahim Ajibade, "Common Online Scams Targeting Teenagers," *Internet Matters*, February 15, 2023. www.internetmatters.org.

"Online Safety," *Nemours Teens Health*, n.d. http://kidshealth.org.

"Phishing: Don't Take the Bait," *Federal Trade Commission*, March 2019. http://consumer.ftc.gov.

WEBSITES

Cyber.org
http://cyber.org

Cyber.org works to educate young people about online safety. Its cybersafety video series provides information about different ways young people can stay safe on the internet.

NetSmartz
www.missingkids.org/netsmartz

Run by the National Center for Missing and Exploited Children, NetSmartz teaches kids and teens how to stay safe online. The website provides information about different types of online dangers and resources to help teens in dangerous situations.

Think Twice Click Once
http://think2click1.com

Think Twice Click Once provides people with tips for staying safe online. The website has information about avoiding online crimes and scams. Its "What Can You Do?" tab provides preemptive ways to stay safe.

INDEX

account numbers, 12
Alicia's Law, 34

Breyault, John, 10, 42

catfishing, 30–31
child sexual abuse material, 11, 24, 28, 31–33, 56
contest scams, 17–18, 41

Daynes, Lewis, 35

Federal Bureau of Investigation, 26, 34
Federal Trade Commission, 38, 52–54
Fraud.org, 10, 38

gift cards, 43
grooming, 27–29, 31, 32–35

Halpert, Ben, 24–26

identity theft, 16–17, 54–55

Kozakiewicz, Alicia, 34

LaFave, Breck, 34–35
LaFave, Lorin, 35
law enforcement, 34, 52, 55–56

malware, 17

Nofziger, Amy, 43

passwords, 12, 15, 51, 52
peer-to-peer payment apps, 43
phishing, 8–9, 14–17, 21, 38–41
phreaks, 15
predators, 10–11, 24–35, 36–38, 44–47, 48, 55–56

scammers, 8–9, 10, 11, 12–23, 38–44, 48, 50–55, 56
scholarship scams, 18–19
shopping scams, 19–21
Social Security numbers, 54–55

Tressler, Colleen, 14
two-factor authentication, 52

usernames, 15

video games, 6–9, 35

Weisman, Steve, 21

IMAGE CREDITS

Cover: © RgStudio/iStockphoto
5: © SuPatMaN/Shutterstock Images
7: © Addictive Stock/iStockphoto
8: © ZikG/Shutterstock Images
9: © ValuaVitaly/iStockphoto
11: © Tero Vesalainen/Shutterstock Images
13: © jmsilva/iStockphoto
14: © ParinPix/Shutterstock Images
16: © Kaspars Grinvalds/Shutterstock Images
19: © Insta_Photos/Shutterstock Images
20: © Christopher Ames/iStockphoto
22: © Pressmaster/Shutterstock Images
25: © Vershinin89/Shutterstock Images
26: © Fast-Stock/Shutterstock Images
27: © SeventyFour/Shutterstock Images
29: © Peerawich Phaisitsawan/Shutterstock Images
30: © Inna Reznik/Shutterstock Images
33: © SolStock/iStockphoto
37: © Ground Picture/Shutterstock Images
39: © Mark Van Scyoc/Shutterstock Images
40: © WinWin Artlab/Shutterstock Images
42: © Tada Images/Shutterstock Images
45: © Monkey Business Images/iStockphoto
47: © F01 Photo/Shutterstock Images
49: © Dobrila Vignjevic/iStockphoto
50: © Kleber Cordeiro/Shutterstock Images
53: © RapidEye/iStockphoto
54: © Richard Stephen/iStockphoto
57: © Studio Romantic/Shutterstock Images

ABOUT THE AUTHOR

Marne Ventura is the author of more than 150 books for young people. A former elementary school teacher, she holds a master's degree in reading and language development from the University of California. Ventura's nonfiction titles cover a wide range of topics, including media literacy, STEM, arts and crafts, food and cooking, biographies, health, history, and survival. Ventura and her family live in California.